Muhammed Goes to the Masjid

Mini Mu'min Du'a Series #9

www.Mini-Mumin.com

Copyright © 2012 Mini Mu'min Publications

All rights reserved. This publication may not be reproduced in whole or in part by any means whatsoever without written permission from the copyright owner.

Introduction

All praise is due to Allah the Most High, may Allah send His blessings on the Prophet Muhammad (saw), his family, his companions, and those who follow him in righteousness until the Day of Judgment.

"And remember your Lord by your tongue and within yourself, humbly and in awe, without loudness, by words in the morning and the afternoon, and be not among those who are neglectful." (Holy Qur'an 7:205)

The **Mini Mu'min Du'a Series** is designed to help you teach your child essential Islamic supplications and the situations in which they would be used. Each book focuses on a single topic, with key vocabulary highlighted. These key words can then serve as a tool to remind your child of important points. All supplications are shown in Arabic text, translation, and transliteration. For any assertions regarding fiqh we have provided textual proofs, from the Qur'an and authentic Sunnah of the Prophet (saw), at the bottom of the relevant page. Each story is accompanied by original artwork, but in accordance with Islamic beliefs we do not use human or animal images.

Transliteration has been provided here as a means to help those who do not know Arabic to teach supplications to their children. But it must be noted that all transliteration is imperfect and cannot accurately represent Arabic sounds in their entirety. We therefore encourage anyone who uses our books to use the transliteration as a tool, but not an end in itself, and to eventually learn the supplications in the original Arabic.

In some cases, sounds will be represented in the transliteration (because they are present in the Arabic text) that will not actually be pronounced. These generally occur at the end of a supplication and are related to the Arabic rules for pausing and stopping. To clarify this for non-Arabic speakers, we have placed brackets [ ] around those sounds in the transliteration that would not be pronounced when reciting the supplication.

Thank you for purchasing this book, may Allah benefit both you and your child through it, forgive us for any errors we have made, and benefit us in this life and the Hereafter if there is any good in it.

Muhammed goes to the Masjid
Each and every day,

Because salaat in **Jamaa'ah**[1]
Is the best way to pray!

You get a **big reward**[2]
For each and every prayer,

That you make sincerely,
While you are there!

---

[1] "Jamaa'ah"- an Arabic word referring to congregational prayer.

[2] Ibn 'Umar (ra) reported: The Messenger of Allah (saw) said, "Prayer in congregation is twenty-seven times more meritorious than a prayer performed individually." (Al-Bukhaari and Muslim)

To get ready-
Muhammed made his **wudoo'**³

And brushed his teeth
With a **siwak**, too.⁴

Then he put on **perfume**-
The very best kind,⁵

Dressed in **clean clothes**⁶
And combed his hair till it shined!

---

³ "Wudoo'"- Ritual purification made before prayer.

⁴ Allah's Messenger (saw) said, "Had it not been difficult for my nation, I would have commanded them to use siwak for every ablution." (Malik) Note: A siwak is a stick from the Arak tree used for brushing the teeth and gums.

⁵ Narrated Anas bin Malik (ra): The Prophet (saw) never refused a gift of perfume.
Note: Indicating the desirability of the use of perfume.

⁶ The Messenger of Allah (saw) said, "Allah does not accept prayer without purity." (Muslim)
Note: This hadith refers to cleanliness (purity) of the body, garment, and place of prayer.

Now he was ready-
He was clean,
He was neat,

He smelled really nice,
And his wudoo' was complete!

Then he walked to the Masjid,
It was not far away,

There is a lot of **reward**[7]
In **walking** to the **Masjid** to pray.

---

[7] Abu Huraira (ra) reported: The Prophet (saw) said, "He who purifies himself (performs wudoo') in his house and then walks to one of the houses of Allah (mosque) for performing an obligatory salaat, one step of his will wipe out his sins and another step will elevate his rank (in Paradise)." (Muslim)

When all of a sudden-
He saw Ibrahim running past...

He called out to his friend,
"Why are you going so fast?"

Ibrahim replied,
(As he stopped for a moment to rest),

"I want to be **on time for prayer**
Because that is best."[8]

---

[8] When the Messenger of Allah (saw) was asked: Which deed is the best? He said, "Performing salaat at its due time." (Muslim)

"Yes, but we don't run to the Masjid,"
Said Muhammed, "this is not a race-

The Masjid is right there,
It's not going anyplace!

Walk calmly when you want
To go to the **Masjid for prayer**,[9]

Don't worry, be patient,
And you will get there."

---

[9] Abu Huraira (ra) reported: I heard the Messenger of Allah (saw) saying, "When the Iqamah (call to prayer) is pronounced, do not come to it running, you should walk calmly with tranquility to join the congregation. Then join in what you catch and complete what you miss." (Al-Bukhaari)

"The Masjid is a very
Special place that we go,

Not rushing is one of the
Rules we must know…"

"There are rules for the Masjid?"
Ibrahim asked with wide eyes.

"Of course," said Muhammed,
"Don't look so surprised!"

Masjid Rules

1.
2.
3.
4.
5.
6.
7.

"When you get to the Masjid
And you go in the door,

Step with your **right foot first**,[10]
Always make sure.

Then, as you go in,
You're not done yet-

Make the **du'a**
for entering the Masjid…
Don't forget!"

---

[10] Aisha (raa) stated: "Allah's Messenger (saw) loved to begin with the right in all his matters, in putting on shoes, in combing his hair, and in purifying himself." (Muslim)

"…one should enter (the mosque) with the right foot…" (*Minhaj Al-Muslim*, Abu Bakr Jabir Al-Jaza'iry)

Du'a Made When Entering the Masjid

أَعُوْذُ بِاللهِ الْعَظِيْمِ، وَ بِوَجْهِهِ الْكَرِيْمِ، وَ سُلْطَانِهِ الْقَدِيْمِ، مِنَ الشَّيْطَانِ الرَّجِيْمِ، بِسْمِ اللهِ، وَ الصَّلَاةُ وَ السَّلَامُ عَلَى رَسُوْلِ اللهِ، اللَّهُمَّ افْتَحْ لِي أَبْوَابَ رَحْمَتِكَ

"A'oodthu billaahil-'adheem, wa bi-wajhihil-kareem, wa sultaanihil-qadeem, minash-shaytaanir-rajeem, bismillaah[i], wassalaatu wassalaamu 'alaa rasoolillaah[i], allaahum-maftah lee 'abwaaba rahmatik[a]."

(I take refuge with Allah, The Supreme, and with His Noble Face, and His eternal authority from the accursed devil.[11] In the name of Allah, and prayers[12] and peace be upon the Messenger of Allah.[13] O Allah, open the gates of Your mercy for me.[14])

---

[11] Abu Dawud, see: *Sahihul-Jaami' As-Saghir* #4591
[12] Ibn As-Sunni #88, and Al-Albaani declared it "Hasan".
[13] Abu Dawud 1/126, see: *Sahihul-Jaami' As-Saghir* 1/528
[14] Muslim 1/494. See also: *Sahih Ibn Maajah* 1/128-9

"Then, once you are in,
Don't sit down right away,

There's a special Sunnah prayer
That we should pray-

Tahiyatul-Masjid,[15]
It's very simple to do…"

"How many raka'aat?" asked Ibrahim.
Muhammed replied, "**Just two**!"[16]

---

[15] "Greeting the Masjid"- a Sunnah prayer made upon entering the Masjid.

[16] Narrated Abu Qatada (ra): The Messenger of Allah (saw) said, "When any one of you enters the mosque, he should perform two raka'aat (of voluntary prayer) before sitting." (Al-Bukhaari and Muslim)

"If someone in the Masjid
Is making their **salaat**,

The area in front of them
Is a very special spot.

Never walk in front,[17]
(It's okay to walk behind)

Of a person who is praying,
Unless their **Sutra**[18] is defined."

---

[17] Narrated Abul-Juhaim bin Al-Harith (ra): The Messenger of Allah (saw) said, "If the person who passes in front of a praying person realizes the enormity of the sinfulness of this act, it will have been better for him to wait for forty than to pass in front of him." (Al-Bukhaari and Muslim) The narrator was not sure whether the Prophet (saw) said forty days, months, or years.

[18] A Sutra is an object like a pillar, wall, stick, spear, etc. that must be in front of a praying person as a symbolic barrier between himself and others. One may walk in front of the Sutra, but not between the praying person and his/her Sutra.

"When it's time for prayer
And everyone is standing up in **rows**,

Make sure to **fill all the gaps**,[19]
Touching shoulders and toes.

If there are any **empty spaces**,
Fill them up nice and tight!

You don't want to leave
Any place for **Shaytaan**, right?"[20]

---

[19] Jabir bin Samurah (ra) reported: The Messenger of Allah (saw) came out to us (once) and said, "Why do you not stand in rows as the angels do before their Rubb (Lord)?" We asked: O Messenger of Allah! How do the angels stand in rows before their Rubb? He (saw) replied, "They complete each row beginning with the first and filling all the gaps." (Muslim)

[20] Narrated Ibn 'Umar (ra): The Messenger of Allah (saw) said, "Arrange the rows in order, stand shoulder to shoulder, close the gaps, be accommodating to your brothers, and do not leave gaps for Satan. Whoever joins up a row, he will be joined to Allah (i.e. to the Mercy of Allah); whoever cuts off a row, he will be cut off from Allah (i.e. from His Mercy)." (Abu Dawud)

"There are special rules for **Friday**
When **Jummah Khutba**[21] has begun-

We don't **play** with anything,[22]
And we don't **talk** to anyone.[23]

So, don't chat with your friends
Or play around with the carpet,

Even if someone else is talking,
You can't even say- 'Stop it!'[24]"

---

[21] "Jummah Khutba"- a religious talk given on Friday, before Jummah prayer.

[22] The Messenger of Allah (saw) said, "Whoever touches the gravel (while the Imam is delivering the Friday sermon) has uttered nonsense, and whoever utters nonsense is considered as if he did not attend the Friday prayer." (Abu Dawud)

[23] Narrated Salman (ra): The Messenger of Allah (saw) said, "If a man takes a bath on Friday, (or) purifies himself as much as he can with wudoo', oils his hair, applies whatever perfume is available in his house, sets forth to the mosque, does not separate two people (to make a seat for himself), performs what is prescribed for him of prayer, and remains silent when the Imam speaks- his (minor) sins between that Friday and the following Friday will be forgiven." (Al-Bukhaari)

[24] The Messenger of Allah (saw) said, "If you say to your companion, 'Be quiet' on Friday, while the Imam is delivering the sermon, then you have uttered nonsense." (Muslim)

"The last two rules for the Masjid
That you must know…

Use your **left foot** for leaving[25]
And make **du'a** as you go."

---
[25] "…he leaves (the mosque) with his left foot first…" (*Minhaj Al-Muslim*, Abu Bakr Jabir Al-Jaza'iry)

Du'a Made When Leaving the Masjid

بِسْمِ اللهِ وَ الصَّلاةُ وَ السَّلامُ عَلَى رَسُولِ اللهِ، اللَّهُمَّ إِنِّي أَسْأَلُكَ مِنْ فَضْلِكَ، اللَّهُمَّ اعْصِمْنِي مِنَ الشَّيْطَانِ الرَّجِيمِ

"*Bismillaah[i] wassalaatu wassalaamu 'alaa rasoolillaah[i], allaahumma innee as'aluka min fudhlika, allaahumm a'simnee minash-shaytaanir-rajeem.*"

(In the name of Allah, and prayers and peace be upon the Messenger of Allah. O Allah, I ask You from your favor. O Allah, guard me from the accursed devil.[26])

---

[26] See footnotes 11-14. See also: *Sahih Kalimat-Tayyib* #48-50

Allaahu-Akbar! Allaahu-Akbar!

By now they had reached the Masjid
And the prayer time had come.

"Those are all the rules,"
Said Muhammed, "we are all done!"

"Jazak-Allah for your help,"
Said Ibrahim, "you really are a friend!"

Then, they went into the Masjid
To pray together…

The End!

Other available titles in the Mini Mu'min Du'a Series:

Batool's Bedtime Story
Bilal's Bakery
Fatimah's First Fasting Day
Jameelah Gets Dressed
Saliha Sneezes
Sheema's Shopping Spree
Waheeda the Wudoo' Wonder
Waleed Wakes Up

and many more!...

Visit our online bookstore at:

www.Mini-Mumin.com

Made in the USA
Charleston, SC
13 January 2014